A SECRET HISTORY OF WORDS

A SECRET HISTORY OF WORDS

Emily Hooton

Illustrated by
Alan Rowe

Collins

Contents

CHAPTER 1
What's so bad about nice?

Has your teacher ever told you not to use the word "nice", but to use something more descriptive instead? Did you ever wonder: what's so bad about nice?

Your teacher is probably on to something. Nice is *all right*, but it's not quite wonderful, superb, glorious or delightful, is it?
You might say to your friend, "That's a nice bag," but wouldn't it be an improvement if you used a more interesting word instead?

Delightful bag, Amelia!

nice If you say that something is nice, you mean that you find it attractive, pleasant or enjoyable.

The word "nice" was a French word that came into the English language in the 1200s. Its roots are from a **Latin** word, *nescius,* meaning foolish or ignorant. The truth is that nice is not so nice, after all! In **Middle English**, it meant stupid and was used as an insult.

3

Knowing that "nice" is an insult really puts a different spin on **idioms** that we use daily.

The words that we use every day hide some incredible secrets about the history of the UK.

You might have noticed that:

English has taken numerous words and phrases from different languages.

Latin Greek Germanic French Norse

So why do we use "nice" to mean that
something is pleasant? And why are we using
a Latin word in English anyway?

The meaning of nice has changed over time,
and what a voyage it's had! From stupid in
1200, to kind and thoughtful in the 1830s, and
to pleasant or agreeable today.

Timeline of "nice"

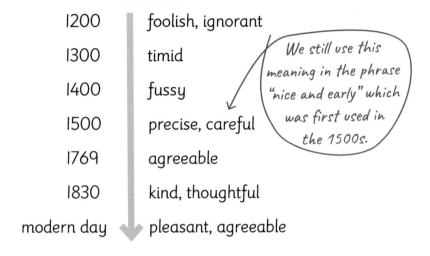

1200	foolish, ignorant
1300	timid
1400	fussy
1500	precise, careful
1769	agreeable
1830	kind, thoughtful
modern day	pleasant, agreeable

We still use this meaning in the phrase "nice and early" which was first used in the 1500s.

But why has the meaning of "nice" changed? Some etymologists think it could be because at different times, small groups of people decided to use the word in a different way. Over time, the new meaning of the word spread.

It's a bit like how some slang words can have a completely different meaning – for example, bad, sick and wicked can all mean good.

> **slang** informal words and expressions used by people who know each other well or who have the same interests

That's just silly!

The word "silly" has had an unusual history

> **silly** foolish, childish or ridiculous

too, but in the other direction to "nice". In the 1200s, it meant to be happy, lucky or blessed.

Timeline of "silly"

1200	happy
1300	innocent
1400	weak
1580	**unsophisticated**
modern day	foolish

By the 1580s the famous poet and **playwright** William Shakespeare used "silly" the way we would now, to mean foolish. But even in one of his plays, "silly" could still have different meanings, such as innocent, frail, plain or unsophisticated.

Back in Shakespeare's time, people used words a little differently and sometimes in a different order. "Fitting well a sheep" means the same as "Fitting a sheep well".

What a muddle!

Weren't all these meanings confusing?
Probably not. If you think about it, we use words
that have more than one meaning all the time.

Homonyms are words that we spell and
pronounce the same way, but that have
different meanings. Because they're used in
different contexts, we don't often get mixed up.
For example, "fly" has different meanings in
these sentences: "Birds can fly," and "A fly
settled on my nose."

How many meanings can you think of for
each of these words?
run   bank   tap   scale

My nose is running!

Contronyms are words that we spell and pronounce the same way, but that have completely different meanings.

wicked – to be very bad *or* to be very good

buckle – to fasten *or* to bend and break

dust – to add fine particles *or* to remove them

left – to have gone *or* something that is remaining

Dust the cake with icing sugar.

CHAPTER 2
The Roman conquest

A whopping 80 per cent of English words are from other languages. But which ones came from Britain originally? We don't know exactly, but not many!

The early settlers were the Celts. They were farmers who grew crops and kept animals for food and clothing. Anything left over would be traded with other tribes. A lot of Celtic words are the names of animals, colours or parts of the landscape.

doe

crag

brock

dun (beige/brown)

Celts lived in simple houses made from wattle and daub. Wattle meant a wooden framework, and daub was a sort of plaster made from mud and straw. The roofs were thatched with straw.

Materials like these don't last long, so we only know the houses were there because there are holes in the ground where the wooden posts were.

Celtic flutes and board game pieces have been discovered, so we know that Celts enjoyed music and games.

It sounds like a simple, happy life. But an army was coming. The Romans. And an army of new words came with them too.

Celtic playing pieces

The Roman Empire stretched across
the whole continent.

Roman Empire **not Roman Empire**

Food for thought

Olive oil, plums, cherries, grapes, leeks, cabbages, rabbits and chickens are a few of the foods that the Romans introduced to Britain.

One reason why the Romans invaded was because Britain had a lot of resources that the Romans wanted.

In 43 CE the Roman army landed in Kent, near Dover. They gradually moved west and north, defeating local Celtic tribes.

This didn't take days, or even weeks – it took them 45 years to reach as far as Scotland. However, they didn't conquer Scotland. Local tribes – the Picts and Scots – fought them off.

The Romans seized lands and took resources like tin, copper and gold. They enslaved the local people and made them work.

The Romans used local workers to build roads.

Celtic leaders realised that they weren't going to beat the Roman army. They made deals with the Romans to try to keep some power.

But not all Celts were happy about the Romans taking over their land. The Iceni tribe, led by queen Boudica, joined forces with other unhappy Celtic tribes. They started a rebellion against the Romans.

Boudica led her troops through the east of England, setting fire to Roman towns and villages on the way. They completely destroyed two major towns, Colchester and London.

The name "Boudica" was a title rather than a name. It meant "she who brings victory". But she was not victorious. The Roman army defeated Boudica's troops and went on to rule England and Wales for 400 years, almost destroying the Celtic way of life.

Back up north

Scottish tribes, the Picts and the Scots, kept attacking the Romans in the north. In 122 CE, Roman Emperor Hadrian ordered troops to build an 80-mile wall to keep the invaders out.

The word "mile" came from a Roman phrase which means "a thousand paces".

How many miles is that?

I've lost count!

Hadrian's Wall

What did the Romans do?

The Romans constructed 20 large towns and 100 smaller ones. The towns were connected by 10,000 miles (16,000 kilometres) of roads.

They introduced plumbing, public baths, laws and large-scale farming. They wrote down their laws, literature and history using Latin.

A third of English words come directly from Latin. The borrowed Latin words were mostly **nouns** describing building materials, food and the army: street, wall, tile, cheese, butter, camp, mile, pound.

camp

Before the Romans, information was passed by **word of mouth**. This is known as an oral tradition. The Celtic leaders *chose* not to write down what they knew so it could be kept safe. This is just like keeping a password safe by remembering it and not writing it down. Some Celts were given the job to remember important information. They also passed information between tribes by word of mouth. If they had used written records, these could have been destroyed by the Romans. This made it difficult for the Romans to wipe out the Celtic way of life.

cheese

wall

LONDINIUM 10 MILES

mile

street

Oral traditions

- Oral tradition is a way of sharing stories and ideas by word of mouth.

- It's still used today by lots of cultures.

- First Nation Australians have been telling the story of how the seas rose after the last Ice Age for 10,000 years, passing it down from generation to generation.

Early humans gathered round a fire listening to a storyteller.

- Storytellers would entertain others by repeating stories that their parents and grandparents had told to them.

- And you've used an oral tradition if you know a nursery rhyme!

"THE CAT AND THE FIDDLE."

Hey diddle, diddle was first printed in 1765, but people had been saying it since at least the 1500s.

Have you ever said a nursery rhyme slightly differently to other people? Different versions of rhymes are passed down through families. You're not wrong, you're the keeper of your family's tradition.

21

CHAPTER 3
Old English is born

The Roman army left Britain in 410 CE to defend their home country of Italy from invaders.

See you later!

When the Romans moved out, Britain was open to attack because it no longer had a large, organised army.

Once the Roman army had gone, there was no one to defend the coast from invaders. Scottish tribes attacked from the north, and Anglo-Saxons invaded from across the sea. Historians think this might be because the sea levels were rising and the Anglo-Saxons' original homes were under water.

The language of the Anglo-Saxons was Anglish and the areas they settled became Angle-land. These were the beginnings of the words "English" and "England". The name given to the language spoken in Britain from about 450 CE is **Old English**.

Why did the Celts start using the new language?

We don't really know, but these are some ideas:

1. The Anglo-Saxons were invited to come and fight off Scottish invaders. The Celts were happy to learn Anglish words so they could speak to their new neighbours.

2. In a few hundred years, there were more Anglo-Saxons than Celts, so their language became the most popular.

3. Some people think that lots of Celts never started using Old English at all. Many Celtic people were pushed out to the furthest corners of Britain and kept using their own languages. This is why Celtic languages are still spoken in Scotland, Wales and Cornwall.

We'll never know exactly how Old English began to be spoken, but it's clear that it was a language that suited the simple Anglo-Saxon way of life.

Old English words were simpler than Latin words, with just one or two syllables. They described everyday life.

Fact

The word "harvest" was used to mean autumn.

thimble
needle
ladle
milk
pin
nail
meat
loaf
wood
bread

A lot of words to describe people come from Anglo-Saxon too: child, daughter, sister, mother, father, brother, friend, man and woman.

The words "mum" and "dad" didn't come along until later, but "ma" and "da" were used. These are the first sounds that babies learn to make.

Food for thought

The Old English word "meat" was used for *any* food. Also, "bread" meant small pieces, or crumbs of any food. "Loaf" was used to describe the baked bread we know today.

What's for lunch, Ma?

Meat and bread.

After a lot of fighting between the Anglo-Saxons, England was split into kingdoms, each with their own ruling king or queen.

We know from gravesites that women could be just as powerful as men. Women could become rulers of a kingdom after their husband died.

The Vikings

Viking ships had been raiding the coast of Britain for 100 years, stealing treasure, food and weapons. In 865, they formed a massive army from across **Scandinavia** and invaded. It's thought that they had scarce resources at home and wanted better farmland.

Vikings were known to be fearsome fighters. They introduced these scary words into English: anger, hit, club, berserk, ransack and … cake.

They came from muddy, swampy countryside, so they also had some good words for the landscape, such as "dirt" and "muck".

All this muck and dirt drives me berserk! I need some cake.

It took 14 years of battles for the Vikings to gain control of the northern half of England. They settled in the north, with York as their capital.

What a muddle!

Before the Vikings, people used the word "he" for he, she, him, her *and* them. This could have been very confusing. The Viking language, Norse, gave us "they", "their" and "them".

Who stole my loaf?

Him!

The Vikings lived side by side with the Anglo-Saxons for 80 years. They gave us names for some of the days of the week, named after their gods:

The god Tyr – Tuesday

Thor – Thursday

Frigg – Friday

Guess which day of the week is named after the god Woden?!

Lots of English words that begin with "sk" or "sc" come from Norse: sky, skin, skill, skull, score and scrub.

He has great skin scrubbing skill!

Fact

Before the Vikings, Anglo–Saxon people used the word "roof" to mean sky, as in "the roof of the world".

Place names

The first part of a place name might come from an important person who lived there, perhaps a man called Dudda. The second part of the name would come from a feature of the landscape, such as a lea, the name for a meadow. These two parts were put together and became Dudda's Lea, or Dudley, as we know it today.

Can you work out what your settlement (or a nearby one) is named after?

Fact

Prefix means added to the beginning of words.

Suffix means added to the end of words.

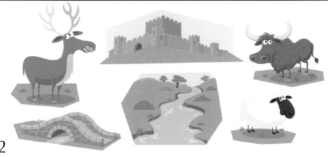

32

Common place name endings

suffix	meaning	place
-ing/ingas	group of people or a clan	Kettering, Wapping
-ham	village	Rotherham, Clapham
-ton/tun	farm	Luton, Southampton
-field	field	Macclesfield, Sheffield
-lea/ley	meadow	Burnley, Bromley
-ford	river crossing	Thetford, Castleford
-mouth	river mouth	Dartmouth, Plymouth
-pool	narrow river inlet	Liverpool, Hartlepool
-burn	brook/stream	Blackburn, Burnside
-chester	fort/castle	Manchester, Colchester
-by	farmstead/village	Busby, Selby, Whitby
-ness	headland	Inverness, Skegness

These prefixes have an animal connection.

prefix	meaning	place
ox-	oxen	Oxford
hart-/buck-	deer	Hartlepool, Buckingham
shep-/skip-	sheep	Shepperton, Skipton

Sutton Hoo treasure

In 1939, an amazing Anglo-Saxon ship was discovered at Sutton Hoo. Under a mound of earth there was an outline of a longship. Experts think it was the grave of a very important warrior because a ship would have been very difficult to put under ground. The warrior was surrounded by gold and silver weapons, bowls, cloth, coins, jewellery, a helmet with a mask, and a shield with gold fittings.

Anglo-Saxons gave us the words grave, helmet, shield and gold.

gold buckle

fitting from a shield

how the gravesite might have looked

shield

helmet

35

CHAPTER 4
Middle English

Some Norse words brought by the Vikings are still used in the north of England and Scotland.

Words like "bairn" (meaning child), "'ey up" (a warning or greeting) and "happen" (meaning perhaps or maybe).

The old Norse word "happ" meant fortune, chance or luck.

How many words can you think of with "hap" in them? These are just a few: happen, mishap and perhaps.

You probably came up with the word "happy" and thought to yourself: "Yes! It *is* good luck to be happy". But how did we get from "hap" to "happy"?

Timeline of "happy"

865	happ, meaning luck
1380s	happy, meaning lucky
1520	happy, meaning greatly pleased

Nowadays, "happy" is an **adjective** – we use it to describe people. But in 1520, "happy" was a verb! If you made someone happy, you could say that you happied them. Why not go and happy someone today?

The Norman conquest

Just as the time of the Vikings and Anglo-Saxons was ending, another invader arrived.

The Anglo-Saxons (ruled by King Harold) and the Vikings (ruled by King Harald) were under attack again. Harold AND Harald? Wasn't that confusing? Don't worry, things were about to get easier!

1066 was a big year in English history. Firstly, Harold defeated Harald at the battle of Stamford Bridge. Harold became king.

Fact

In 1066, an enormous long-tailed comet was visible in the sky. People were very superstitious and saw this as bad luck for King Harold.

King Harold

It *was* bad luck. King Harold was defeated by William of Normandy at the Battle of Hastings. William I became the first king of all England. He became known as William the Conqueror.

But there was a problem.
William the Conqueror didn't speak the same
language as the people who lived in the country
he'd just taken over. William and his followers
spoke French, and they wrote laws and other
documents in French and Latin. So the local
people suddenly faced a barrage of new words
they didn't understand. Over time, though,
words from French began to enter English.
People picked useful French words to bring into
what was now called Middle English.

40

The new French words were often more formal or fancy than words that were used in Old English. In England, you lived in a house. This could be a tiny hut or a large house, but it was still called a house. When the Normans arrived, this house could be called a mansion or a manor.

Food for thought

New ways of cooking arrived from France, and so did new words for food. Basic Anglo-Saxon "meat" was replaced with words like beef, mutton, venison and poultry. Rather than just bake or roast, you could now fry, grill or broil food. Plain old English "sop" became fancy French "soup".

Well, that's terrific!

terrific extremely good

The word "terrific" is another word that has had an extraordinary voyage. In 1066, the blazing comet in the sky was looked at in terror by Anglo-Saxons. Just think about looking up at the sky and seeing a giant fireball and not knowing how it came to be there. You would probably think that something terrifying was coming!

The word "terror" was a French word from an original Latin root meaning "frighten". William the Conqueror and the Normans introduced this word into English. The same Latin root made the words "deter" and "deterrent" meaning to scare off.

In the 1380s, the word "terrible" came along. It meant something that *caused* terror.

The word "terrific" started to be used in the 1660s to mean causing terror.
 By the 1920s, "terrific" was used with other words to make them stronger, a bit like using huge or enormous. It meant an intense or very strong feeling. For example, you could make a terrific noise or there might be a terrific storm.

Slowly, the word "terrific" jumped from meaning something very bad to something very good. For example, you could see a terrific sunset.

Today, terrific is used to describe something that is excellent or extremely good.

Timeline of "terrific"

1000		terror, frightening
1380		terrible, causing fear
1660		terrific, causing fear
1920s		an intense feeling, making a noun stronger
today		very good

Terrific bag, Amelia!

CHAPTER 5
Middle to Modern English

Middle English sounded much more like the English we know today. It was still difficult to read, though, because there were lots of dialects and spellings.

Fact

Dialects are the different ways people speak in different parts of the country.

Not many people could read, anyway. There were some schools, run by monks. They taught Latin, maths and religion. Only children from well-off families could learn to read. But *what* was there to read?

Early **manuscripts** were copied by **scribes** and written out by hand using ink pens.

The pages often had beautiful pictures. What if the scribe made a mistake? They'd have to start again! Because books were written by hand, there weren't many copies and they were very expensive.

Doodles

Some of the first doodles came from scribes testing their ink pens on the margins before writing. These were known as "marginalia". They drew pictures of people, squiggly lines or even knights fighting snails!

The word "doodle" didn't come into English until much later and meant foolish. Doodles were foolish drawings. The word "doodle" might partly come from the word "dawdle" meaning to be slow.

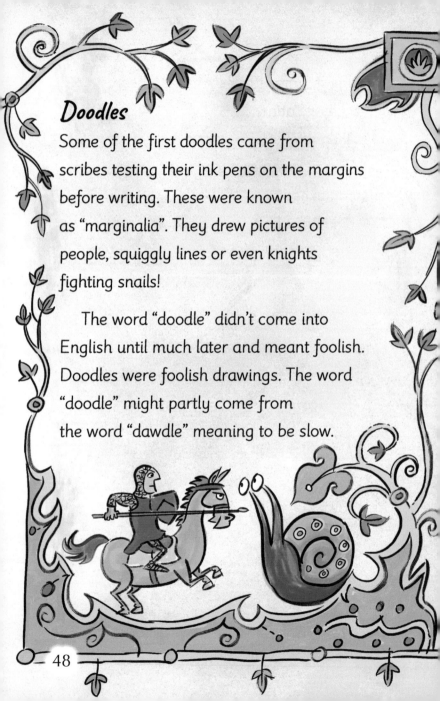

The first writer to use Middle English instead of French or Latin was **Chaucer**. His most famous book, written between 1387 and 1400, was about a group of **pilgrims** travelling on a long expedition. Back then, a trip like this would have been a great adventure. On the way, each pilgrim in the group tells the other pilgrims a tale. Lots of the tales were funny or had a lesson for the reader.

Fact

Chaucer made up the word "twitter" to describe the sounds of birds chirping. He was also the first to use the words "galaxy" and "magician".

Printing books

In 1476, William Caxton introduced the **printing press** to England. It was a machine with metal letters that were arranged to make words and sentences. Ink was then added and paper pressed on top. Being able to print lots of copies of books made them cheaper, so many more people could read them. Caxton translated lots of manuscripts into English. He used a single dialect from London, which helped to simplify spelling.

The spellings of some words got changed by mistake. Caxton put an "h" into the English word "gost", creating "ghost". The same mistake changed "gastly" to "ghastly" and "agast" to "aghast".

Shifting sounds

Have you ever wondered why "food" and "good" are spelled the same way, but pronounced differently? Well, here's something to boggle your mind: in Middle English they *were* pronounced the same way and would have rhymed with "toad".

Mmm, goad foad!

In the Middle Ages, something amazing was happening. It wasn't just how we *spelt* words that was changing, but how we *said* them. This was called the great vowel shift.

In Middle English:

"cow" was pronounced "coo"

"bite" was pronounced "beet"

"to" was pronounced "toe"

"meet" was pronounced "mate"

and people pronounced the "g" in "enough" and the "k" and "g" in "knight".

Caxton and the printing press came in the middle of this shifting of sounds. The way we pronounce vowels today was fixed by about 1700. However, there was a huge number of printed books by then. Changing the spelling in those books to match the new way sounds were said would have been an enormous job. So, we still use the old spellings like "enough" and "knight" today.

Shakespeare's English

By **Elizabethan** times, both spoken and written English would have been easy to understand.

William Shakespeare, a great poet and playwright, wrote in **Early Modern English**. He was born in Stratford upon Avon in 1564, during the reign of Queen Elizabeth I.

Shakespeare wrote around 38 plays including *Romeo and Juliet, Hamlet* and *Macbeth*. A lot of people think that he is the greatest writer in the history of the English language. Although you might not have seen a Shakespeare play, you'll know some phrases from Shakespeare that we still use today.

And he made up 420 words! Cheap, excitement, fashionable and majestic are all Shakespeare's.

CHAPTER 6

English today

The main way English has changed since Shakespeare's time is that lots of new vocabulary has been added. People began to travel and bring words back with them.

From the 1500s, the British Empire grew in a similar way to the Roman Empire. The British wanted more land so that they could have more power and wealth. They seized lands and resources. Sometimes, the British enslaved some of the people who were living in the lands they seized. The British also got rich by selling resources they got from these countries.

Britain **colonised** places all around the world, including America, Australia, New Zealand, India, Pakistan and some African countries.

English came to be spoken around the globe. When countries took back their independence, some still spoke their own versions of English.

With all of these versions of English around the world, lots of new words entered the language.

English-speaking areas

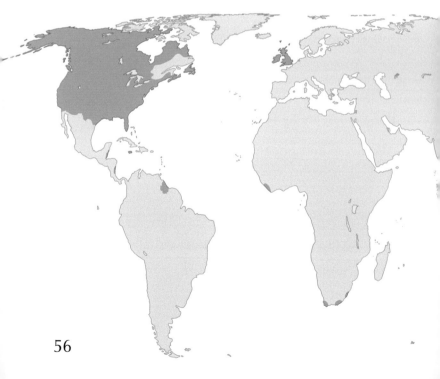

Food for thought

As British travellers went around the world, they tried new foods. They took some of these to England.

- potatoes and tomatoes from Mexico
- bananas and yams from Gambia and Nigeria
- coffee from Turkey
- tea from China
- curry from India

What a muddle!

When British explorers asked local people the name of a river, the reply was often "river" in the local language. Explorers sometimes thought the word they heard was the name of the river and added it to the map! The Malopo River in South Africa means "River River".

Expanding vocabulary

Some writers thought that using Latin and Greek
would make their writing feel more important.
They made up complicated words, borrowing
from Latin and Greek. For example, one new
word was "encyclopedia", meaning a book of
information on lots of topics. This came from two
Greek words: *enkyklios* meaning circular and
pedia meaning education.

As new things were invented, people borrowed
more Latin and Greek to make up new words.

The photograph was invented in the 1830s. Photographs use light to make a picture. So two Greek words – *photo* meaning light, and *graph* meaning drawing or writing – were put together to name the new invention.

Television was invented in 1927. The word *tele* was Greek for far away and *vis* comes from the Latin to see. "Television" means a machine for seeing things that are far away!

Can you guess what the word "telephone" means?

Fact

If you see a word starting with "ph" then it's probably Greek in origin. Philosophy, phone, photo, phobia and physics are all based on Greek words.

You might think that the word "computer" is modern, but it has been used in English since Shakespeare's time. It meant a *person* who did calculations.

The first machine that could do calculations was invented in 1821 by Charles Babbage. It wasn't like the computers we know today, but it could be programmed. Ada Lovelace was the first computer programmer.

Other computing machines were made, and some of them filled a whole room! In the 1940s, people thought that the whole world would only ever need five computers.

Machines a bit like the computers we use now were developed in the 1970s and 1980s. Tablets and mobile phones today are more powerful than those early computers.

The internet

Just over 30 years ago, the internet was invented. How did people find information before the internet? They had to go to a library and look in books!

What are you doing?

Googling!

Now you can use the internet to find out all kinds of information from anywhere in the world. It's no wonder that words and phrases are passed around and change meanings so quickly.

Words like "selfie" and "lol" have become everyday vocabulary.

English is dynamic – this means that it's always changing. The internet has made it much easier for English to develop. Words are being added all the time. A new word in 2022 was "splooting". It describes an animal lying flat on its tummy with its legs stretched out.

Splooting is a mix of splay, splat and scoot!

So, we've finally arrived at **Modern English**. Or just plain old English – but you now know that it's not so plain after all! And now it's up to you and your generation to take English on its next adventure!

Words from around the world

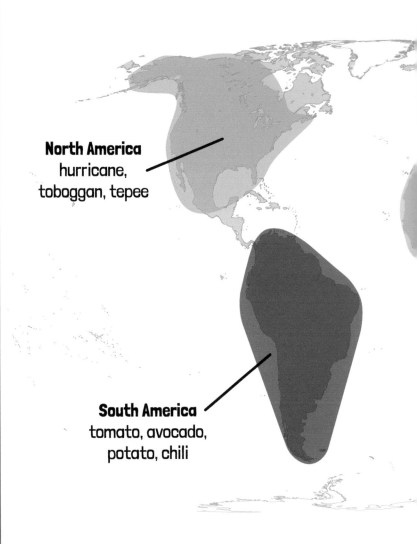

North America
hurricane,
toboggan, tepee

South America
tomato, avocado,
potato, chili

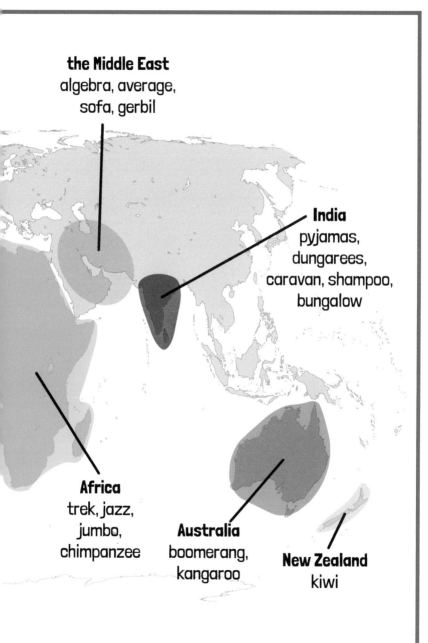

the Middle East
algebra, average,
sofa, gerbil

India
pyjamas,
dungarees,
caravan, shampoo,
bungalow

Africa
trek, jazz,
jumbo,
chimpanzee

Australia
boomerang,
kangaroo

New Zealand
kiwi

65

Greek and Latin roots

Some inventions that were named using Greek and Latin root words are thermometer, telescope and microscope. Try making up your own words using these Greek and Latin roots.

For example, an "aquatherm" could be a new sort of kettle!

You might find that you come up with words you already know!

Greek roots

anti – against

auto – self

chrome – colour

photo – light

bio – life

micro – small

graph – drawing

therm – heat

phobia – fear

tele – far away

scope – to look

sub – under

logy – to study

techno – skill or art

Latin roots

aqua – water

audio – to hear

dict – to say

manu – hand

multi – many

port – to carry

vis/vid – to see

motio – motion/move

doc – teach

scrib/script – to write

Terrific "manuport" Amelia!

Glossary

adjective a describing word

Chaucer a writer who lived from 1340–1400

colonised when a country takes control of
another country

Early Modern English a form of English
spoken between about 1500 and 1700

Elizabethan during the rule of
Queen Elizabeth I (1558–1603)

idioms well-known phrases that mean
something different to their literal meaning,
e.g. "raining cats and dogs"

Latin a language that was used in
ancient Rome

manuscripts handwritten books or documents

Middle English a form of English spoken
between about 1150 and 1500

Modern English a form of English spoken between about 1700 and today.

noun a word that is the name of something

Old English a form of English spoken between about 450 and 1150

pilgrims travellers on a trip to a special place.

playwright a person who writes plays

printing press a machine that prints books

Scandinavia the countries Norway, Denmark and Sweden

scribes people who copy documents by hand

unsophisticated simple

word of mouth passing information from person to person by speaking

About the author

How did you get into writing?

I've always enjoyed writing and
started more seriously when
a friend challenged me to write
a novel in a month.

Emily Hooton

**What do you hope readers
will get out of the book?**

I hope readers will learn a little bit
about English and think about the words they use in
a different way.

What is it like for you to write?

It's a bit like doing a complicated puzzle, trying to put all
the pieces in the right places. Sometimes it takes a while
for them to slot together, but they do in the end.

**What is a book you remember loving reading
when you were young?**

I remember liking *Stig of the Dump* and *Flat Stanley*, but
I loved *Watership Down*, by Richard Adams.

Why did you write this book?

I am really interested in the origins of words and am always looking up where they came from. I realised I'd got a lot of (some might say useless) facts together – that's why I decided to write the book.

What word do you like best? Why?

Vermilion. It's the name of a particular shade of red. It comes from a Latin word "vermis" which means worm! I like it because it fills up your mouth when you say it – in a way you really wouldn't want worms to do!

Are there any words you don't like? Why?

I don't like the word "nice". It means so many different things and most of them aren't nice at all!

What was the funniest thing you found out when researching this book?

I love that the words "good" and "food" used to be pronounced the same way and that they rhymed with "toad". It makes me want to shake my fist at English for being so difficult.

About the illustrator

What made you want to be an illustrator?

I loved watching cartoons as a child. Daffy Duck, Droopy and Wacky Races to name a few. When I wasn't watching cartoons or playing football, I spent most of my spare time drawing. I remember one of my

Alan Rowe

teachers catching me doodling during a lesson and telling me "You won't earn a living drawing silly pictures!" I think that inspired me to show they were wrong. Drawing silly pictures for a living seemed like a fantastic idea!

How did you get into illustration?

Art was by far my best subject at school. After my A-Levels I gained a place at art college, which led me into illustration.

What did you like best about illustrating this book?

I always enjoy adding some silliness to characters and events from the past. It's a bit like rewriting history!

What was the most difficult thing about illustrating this book?

Working out what people wore and how things looked back in the day. They didn't have cameras back then!

Is there anything in this book that relates to your own experiences?

I remember Halley's Comet appearing back in 1986 and thinking I'll be dead or incredibly old the next time it comes around.

How do you bring a character to life in an illustration?

Exaggerated, humorous facial expression are the key for me, especially in my cartoony style.

Which word do you like best?

I like 'yes' the most. It's the most positive word I can think of, it's also easy to spell.

What's the most interesting thing you found out while illustrating this book?

Before the Vikings, people used the word "he" for he, she, him, her and them. That's interesting!

Book chat

What did you think of the book at the start? Did you change your mind as you read it?

If you could ask the author one question, what would it be?

What was the most exciting/interesting thing you learnt from reading the book?

What do you think the illustrations add to this book?

Did it surprise you to find out that the English language is always changing?

Which part of the book did you like best, and why?

How do you think English might change in the future?

Which word's history did you find the most interesting?

Book challenge:

Pick a word you like. Look online or in a dictionary to find out where the word came from.

Collins
BIG CAT

Published by Collins
An imprint of HarperCollins*Publishers*

The News Building
1 London Bridge Street
London SE1 9GF
UK

Macken House
39/40 Mayor Street Upper
Dublin 1
D01 C9W8
Ireland

10 9 8 7

ISBN 978-0-00-862475-0

British Library Cataloguing-in-Publication Data
A catalogue record for this publication is available
from the British Library.

Download the teaching notes and
word cards to accompany this book at:
http://littlewandle.org.uk/signupfluency/

Get the latest Collins Big Cat news at
collins.co.uk/collinsbigcat

Author: Emily Hooton
Illustrator: Alan Rowe
Publisher: Lizzie Catford
Product manager and commissioning
   editor: Caroline Green
Series editor: Charlotte Raby
Development editor: Catherine Baker
Project manager: Emily Hooton
Content editor: Daniela Mora Chavarría
Copyeditor: Sally Byford
Phonics reviewer: Rachel Russ
Proofreader: Gaynor Spry
Typesetter: 2Hoots Publishing Services Ltd
Cover designer: Sarah Finan
Production controller: Katharine Willard

Collins would like to thank the teachers and
children at the following schools who took part in
the trialling of Big Cat for Little Wandle Fluency:
Burley And Woodhead Church of England Primary
School; Chesterton Primary School; Lady Margaret
Primary School; Little Sutton Primary School;
Parsloes Primary School.

Printed and bound in the UK

MIX
Paper | Supporting
responsible forestry
FSC
www.fsc.org
FSC™ C007454

Acknowledgements
The publishers gratefully acknowledge the
permission granted to reproduce the copyright
material in this book. Every effort has been made
to trace copyright holders and to obtain their
permission for the use of copyright material.
The publishers will gladly receive any information
enabling them to rectify any error or omission at the
first opportunity.

p20 Sheila Terry/Science Photo Library, p21 19th
era/Alamy Stock Photo, p34l The Print Collector/
Alamy Stock Photo, p34r The Print Collector/Alamy
Stock Photo, p35t Heritage Image Partnership Ltd/
Alamy Stock Photo, p35bl SPK/Alamy Stock Photo,
p35br The National Trust Photolibrary/Alamy Stock
Photo, p47 GRANGER – Historical Picture Archive/
Alamy Stock Photo.